LOS ANGELES

ALSO BY M. L. WILLIAMS

Other Medicines
How Much Earth: The Fresno Poets (co-editor)

GAME

GAME

M. L. WILLIAMS

LOS ANGELES

Copyright © 2021 by M. L. Williams. All rights reserved.
Published in the United States by What Books Press,
the imprint of the Glass Table Collective, Los Angeles.

Library of Congress Cataloging-in-Publication Data

Names: Williams, M. L., 1959- author.
Title: Game / M. L. Williams.
Description: Los Angeles : What Books Press, [2021] | Summary: "Game is a
   work of poems, many triggered by the philosophical language of
   Wittgenstein, exploring the catastrophe of language through loss, love,
   and play"-- Provided by publisher.
Identifiers: LCCN 2021023510 | ISBN 9781733378970 (paperback)
Subjects: LCGFT: Poetry.
Classification: LCC PS3623.I558595 G36 2021 | DDC 813/.6--dc23
LC record available at https://lccn.loc.gov/2021023510

Cover art: Gronk, *Untitled*, mixed media on paper, 2021
Book design by Ash Good, www.ashgood.com

What Books Press
363 South Topanga Canyon Boulevard
Topanga, CA 90290

WHATBOOKSPRESS.COM

For Alice

CONTENTS

I. THE WORLD IS ALL

Winter Morning	15
Ceci N'est Pas Un Pot	16
Van Ness	17
Kite	18
Writing Spider (Argiope Aurantia)	19
Fungus Suite	20
Hate The Moon	22
Summer Thunderstorm	23
Pile	24
La Vie Conjugale	25
Vermeer	26
Roast	27

II. WHAT THE FALL IS

Ixchel	31
Nit	32
Desire	33
Hunahpu: Panhandle, San Francisco, 1982	34
Shezmu	35
Ila	36
Marduk	38
Spes	39

Harpocrates	40
Sud	41
Xiuhtecuhtli	42
Wendover	43
Sub Rosa	44
Euryphaessa	45
Stations Of The Cross	46

III. WHAT YOU CANNOT SAY

Hat	49
Calliopes	50
Élevage	51
Fear Of Water, 19Ø3	52
Bone Wine	53
Thoth	54
The Temple	55
Looking For Café Midi: Fresno, 1983	60
Last Aubade	61
Too Much	62

IV. YOU MUST GIVE

Game	65
EI w''''(x) − (H + h(w)) w''(x) + q /H h(w) = p(x) ∀x∈ (0, L)	66
The Uncertainty Principle	67
Blue	68
Late	69
A Side Of Love	70

Intrasocial Disunity In Neoliberal Economies	72
You Must Change Your Life	73
Suwannee Watershed	74
Saint Augustine	75

V. TO SILENCE

Quiet Night	79
Circuit	80
Escalante	81
Utah	82
High Desert	83
Virga	84
Nor Spanish Nor Moss	85
Late Thunderstorm	86
Winter Night	87

ENVOI

Slab!	91

Notes	93
Acknowledgments	96

I.
THE WORLD IS ALL

WINTER MORNING

> I can easily imagine someone always doubting before he opened
> his front door whether an abyss did not yawn behind it . . .
> —Ludwig Wittgenstein, *Philosophical Investigations*, 84

Rinse the coffee cup,
set it in the sink
beside the crumbed plate,
adjust your dark
collar, your coat, your
phone, yes, sun
in the back window
a flood off the late
winter snow, flood
of light and you know
it will be cracking
cold, the icicles yet
to find their slow drip,
light a blue trick
like a surgeon's lamp
when the anesthesia
wears off, to go out
and clear the driveway,
to scrape the glass
through halos of breath,
each magpie a night
in itself beyond
the stone threshold,
its burden of pain,
but first, the door.

CECI N'EST PAS UN POT

> But what if one insisted on saying that there must also be
> something boiling in the picture of the pot?
> —Ludwig Wittgenstein, *Philosophical Investigations*, 297

i.

The old forger might have laughed,
had he lived long enough to see
his youthful face on the 500 franc note,
recalling, after the war, printing his own
bank notes, painting fake Picassos,
adding de Chirico town squares to the mounting sum
of de Chirico squares just to stay alive.
"This is," he might have said, "my face."
"This," he might have said, "is not my face."

ii.

"What is in the pot, Rene?"
Sheila coyly asks. Steam
rises, or perhaps blows
a fierce whistle. He
has planned all afternoon
to offer her a cup of tea
with sugar or a boiled
potato with butter and salt,
to keep her a little longer—
his wife away on social calls—
to talk of art, or nothing at all.
"Nothing," he answers. "It is just
my upturned derby pouring out
desire. It is just the river Sambre,
where my mother drowned."

VAN NESS

> But do you know of such a shadow?
> —Ludwig Wittgenstein, *Philosophical Investigations*, 194

Elongated shade
of a quiet room, map
on the wall pinned
and starred, the table,
its cup, its
folded napkin,
seizure of sunlight
rhombusing the tile,
and you, long
and leaning, framed
in it, light
enough to read
then shadow
enough, machine
of the book,
my hand turning
a page out
of its darkness,
refrigerator hum
over house wrens
in the bougainvillea
then wrens in
the bougainvillea, then
your quiet hello,
your gift of paper
towels and milk
beside the empty
cup, the light
under the fan
screwing its grey cross
ever into the ceiling.

KITE

> But isn't *the same* at least the same?
> —Ludwig Wittgenstein, *Philosophical Investigations*, 215

Swallow-tailed kite, all four-foot wingspan,
page-white head, ink black back,
rises from a tree above the backyard wall,
rises from a nest of mockingbirds there,
two at its scissor tail, too late, too small
to make it drop the fluff in its talons
as it veers and soars, bird eating bird in flight.

WRITING SPIDER (ARGIOPE AURANTIA)

> We feel as if we had to repair a torn spider's web with our fingers.
> —Ludwig Wittgenstein, *Philosophical Investigations*, 106

Night in her tangles, sticky warp a luna
moth reads wrong through deck lights,

hunger and prey, her name a child's
lightning zigzag she sits on, trembling

black and yellow, fist-sized Calypso
winding gold threads branch to ground—

six feet, ten feet—elaborate shuttle
in gorgeous slow dance up and down

into *come to me* orb after orb and they come,
invisible ink to the leafhopper bounding

through privet, hunger and prey
and in Tennessee they say she'll count

your teeth if you smile nearby, write
in her web the years she reckons

you have left to live in this worldly
maze she won't lead you out of,

though you trace her every line.

FUNGUS SUITE

> A main cause of philosophical disease—a one-sided diet . . .
> —Ludwig Wittgenstein, *Philosophical Investigations*, 593

i. Porcini Weather

Little pigs the earth gives up
to butter in my pan, I ransack
ground for *cepes*, king bolete,
Steinpilz or penny bun, *panza*
or *prawdziwek—boletus edulis*.

Dull button hidden under mulch
at first, it domes, blossoms weird
and phallic early in hot autumn,
spreads loaf-like and springy, fist-fat,
bay brown, pocked and bug-holed,
snail-tracked and maggot scurfy,
earwig home before it dies
into its sporey afterlife
of slime, unless I find it
first and slice it into risotto
or fettucini carrettierra,
porcini and wine on seared
rare rib-eye, or dried and saved
to bring a hint of earth to soup.

ii. Oyster

Log in the damp woods, beetle-wracked, slug-licked,
bark flaking into dark soil near the slow creek,
yet white wings small as nickles push out
to grow big as hands and spread and lift

into the canopy, it seems, if these were wings.
Closer, the fanning clusters hang ripe with fungus
flies and tiny beetles I have to rinse out
before I can mince them, fry them with rice
and garlic, peas and carrots and scallions,
lovely side oyster toothy as meat,
but soy, oak, and sesame in the mouth,
fire from a bird's eye and you
across from me, chopsticks ready.

iii. Destroying Angel

Such pure white you think it holds sun
to lamp the forest floor along
whatever needle-
paved path you're walking
this late, whatever pilgrimage
beneath the pines and summer
stars over meadows, Wiccan
rites, or skinny
dipping in the pond.

If beauty is the beginning
of terror, this is what he meant,
for one, picked, mistaken
for a meadow mushroom,
can make one foraged dish
into a last supper
fit for a Roman emperor
or day hikers out for pure air
and something wild in the pan.

HATE THE MOON

> *This* is the face he shews the world . . .
> —Ludwig Wittgenstein, *Philosophical Investigations*, 606

Frost-white face cools nothing, its notional sadness, that we call it a face, call it man when its move is for menses, liar moon, dark side mocking, its slit-eyed cinema trick, its tidal drag up long estuaries and out, omens us and cuckolds, shimmers waves in long stabbing angles, that it insists poetically, moth light and held breath, hunter and fall blues moon and owl-eyed, sad music, cotton-white and boll-pricked moon, voyeur moon, oh cliché moon, plague and cotillion moon, brass band under a hurricane sky pickpocket moon, Hecate's hounds after you moon, morning rise and wine dregs moon, its gibbous promise raising a sigh, August robed in smoke and ash, gilt in smog, slow-in-its-arc moon, eclipse moon color of bad teeth, oh, hot, this ever long night be done.

SUMMER THUNDERSTORM

Sunshine around the clouds doles no comfort. Nimbus mushrooms—I want to say *atomic*—rises, spreads, blossoms like roses on old Disney shows Sunday nights before cold war bedtime. Rains through the shine and they say around here *the devil's beating his wife*. They say around here *y'all are welcome honey* or *that neighborhood is mixed. Smothered and covered*. Will wash it out and the lightning cracks through, terrible light. Terrible light. Burn leaf piles and ropes of smoke trouble oak branches. *We don't talk about that*. Loud when it breaks but it cools and the roads steam and the ditches run. *Bless your heart* they say.

PILE

> . . . the cow chews its food and then dungs the rose with it . . .
> —Ludwig Wittgenstein, *Philosophical Investigations*, II, xi

Avocado trees and sweet potato vines
erupt from little mounds behind
the playhouse where the compost goes—

banana peels, "sour dead" of lime
and lemon rinds, coffee grounds, molding
onion skins, potatoes, garlic, blood

of beets, wilting yellowed kale, carrot
peels, cilantro in *kobicha* liquefaction,
all impasto under a cluster of flies

the green anoles catch. Wild rose,
its "teeth in the mouth of a beast," blossoms
under knives of lemongrass, thatch of smilax

climbing the empty doghouse thorn by thorn—
all corruption, this green riot I trip over
after a few sharp tongues of scallions, to pinch

them off, slice them, dress lamb vindaloo
over saffroned basmati with their green O's.

LA VIE CONJUGALE

> A *picture* held us captive.
> —Ludwig Wittgenstein, *Philosophical Investigations*, 115

A man in the background facing the viewers of Vuillard's painting and looking slightly to his left stands before a window, night, lamps gold and algae green on an obscured building blazing to his left, a muntin seeming to impale his head from the top, another through his waist from jamb to jamb, as though he is hung on an upturned cross. He wears a warm coat. The drapes—two tall rectangles of small green squares, forest green and dark olive, stacked on either side—contain him, squeeze him. His beard swallows his face. He is already gone.

A woman sits left of him in the foreground, from the viewers' angle, facing right in profile before the rectangle of a closed door. She is engulfed in brown and the brown shadow of a chair lost in it, her hands dug into her green lap. She stares past the table before her and slightly down at its burden of cups and a riot of green squares on the tablecloth that match and refuse to match the drapes, and the hint of a green bottle. And behind her the wallpaper—bruised by flowers and stems, dull purples, bland greens, red smears, like a kidney cross section on a slide—looms. The apparition of another chair floats between them. No floor holds anything up, just brown and brown. She sits buried in the paler green rectangles of her dress, the bright red slash of her blouse a wound in the painting, its rectangles the graves of its viewers, still young, holding hands.

VERMEER

> —But a face in a *painting* looks at us too.
> —Ludwig Wittgenstein, *Philosophical Investigations*, II, vi

No, not the Vermeer who painted a woman,
Head tilted into light as she pours light
Into a milkbowl beside bread, not the Vermeer
Who painted the young woman you walk toward,
Her eyes wide, lips parted, because she wants you
To come closer so you can see yourself
In the shining globe of her earring dangling,
Not the Vermeer whose uncertain young woman
Dressed in red silk seeks your advice
About the wine a man urges her to drink
While brooding Temperance looks on.
Drink the wine, you say. But this isn't about
The Vermeer of Delft. This is about
The Vermeer of Pella, Iowa, the Vermeer
Of trenchers and tree chippers and stump cutters,
The Vermeer of tub grinders and power mulchers,
Of hay balers and core saws and rock drills,
The Vermeer sitting yellow and abandoned,
Glistening beside the highway Sunday
As you speed past, the Vermeer on Monday
Hard at work when traffic stalls
And you crawl past close and she
Adjusts her hardhat and looks right at you
As the branch she releases becomes,
In this beatific morning light, dust.

That Vermeer.

ROAST

> Describe the aroma of coffee.—Why can't it be done?
> —Ludwig Wittgenstein, *Philosophical Investigations*, 610

Chocolate and a bitter touch of tar horn through the fog
of steamed milk and brown sugar, giant cap at Cafe Roma,
Berkeley, dark in a pilsner pint glass, awake all night.

High notes of dark chocolate, hazelnut, smoky kumquat
meet Papa's opera notes in the Cafe Trieste,
North Beach, caffeinating the poems of the beats.

Smooth, rich carob and caramel, sweet with its haunt
of jasmine tea in light roast Altura Chiapas served black,
with chile verde and cotija on eggs with tortillas, Cancun.

Deep wild elephant dung musk and chocolate syrup funk,
a dank Seattle roast on Queen Anne's Hill;
knowing Shakespeare trivia is worth a quarter off.

Medium cocoa and sweet bright berry break the heart
the barista draws into foam at the Palomino, Sydney,
smashed avo and toast with poached egg before we walk.

The endless cup metallic, hint of vanilla when fresh
on the road through Little Rock, Waffle House pork chops,
eggs over easy, hash browns covered, chunked, smothered.

Ludwig stalls over his melange at the Cafe Central,
three brothers dead by suicide, a war lost,
the proposition of this perfect cup—no words.

II.
WHAT THE FALL IS

IXCHEL

> It is like looking into the cabin of a locomotive.
> —Ludwig Wittgenstein, *Philosophical Investigations*, 12

The train's horn doesn't belie my nervousness. Safe in my home, I feel its swaying mass, its clatter, its cone of light marked by rain into bright blur, gleaming tracks steaming in its aftermath, what it carries through and out of town and who rides furtively over the rocks and ties, paints on the galvanized walls, bright names, brief politics, a flaking veneer of souls just looking for a ride, blanketing the enterprise of *is* that would otherwise connect nothing to nothing, secret cargo to secret cargo, horn to crossing signal, boxcar to tanker uncoupled and unloaded in the yard, what's carried across but not emptied into bills of lading—the names on the side in bright wide letters tall as I might be if mine were painted in seafoam and cobalt, the picture of the sad girl with straight, black hair looking down at her hand always, what she sees there.

NIT

> And the strength of the thread does not reside in the fact that some one fibre runs through its whole length, but in the overlapping of many fibres.
> —Ludwig Wittgenstein, *Philosophical Investigations*, 67

The pond burns itself into the air above it, which spins out slow through the pasture, up toward water oaks laced with moss, toward slash pine, fat-branched gums. Hard to breathe all that wet, that cow giving its tongue a turn around the lick, sun dead center in the pond weaving a runner of blindness if you look long enough at it trying to see that gator hiding in its bright shatter and eyeing that milk-heavy cow like it remembers something. Pitchfork tine and its one slow note when you pluck it like a bowstring. Loose ends all afternoon and no name for any of it but quiet.

DESIRE

> But here it is an important fact that I imagined a deity in order to imagine this.
> —Ludwig Wittgenstein, *Philosophical Investigations*, 346

Cuttlebone and seed, mirror and perch,
toy bells to peck and rattle, long reed frame
of your cage, branch to the floor and the door
open and Rati takes you out, kisses the bow
of your beak and scratches your head

while you say nothing and say nothing
when Kamadeva calls her back to bed
and she naked returns to him naked
to kiss and embrace elaborately, awkwardly,
cry of pain, cry of pleasure, bees

at every blossom, and you know the words
and fly to the curtain and stare with your black
and gold eye, you know the words and fly
to the book on the table and say nothing,
parrot, you say nothing until he is made ash,

until she, holding his sugarcane bow, his quiver
of arrows, howls in grief. Then, parrot, speak.

HUNAHPU: PANHANDLE, SAN FRANCISCO, 1982

> . . . because in another sense he is already master of a game.
> —Ludwig Wittgenstein, *Philosophical Investigations*, 31

The burnt taste of Thunderbird rains hot
down the throat even on this cool day
in Golden Gate Park, where you live today,

where you hold out a bottle to share
a little kick from heaven. After all,
you've just kicked my young ass playing

basketball, and, tall and athletic as I am,
I didn't think you could make the sky
rain sweet threes past the top of the key,

not missing the index finger on your shooting
hand, not with old, pants-bound legs—
fake left, cross, step back—the *shhh*

of the fraying net tracking your points
and I can't do anything but watch
because today, your game is beautiful.

Sometimes the world's too much, but not
today. Sun burns fog into bright haze,
and this game and you and the park

are enough, our sweat steaming the wet, cool air.
So I say the only thing there is to say:
"Good game, man. Thank you for the wine."

SHEZMU

> Equally there are feelings of strangeness.
> —Ludwig Wittgenstein, *Philosophical Investigations*, 596

Juke blues jangle the glasses
lined up along the wet walnut
bar and thump resonance waves
concentric in this wine glass
set not on, but beside the powder
blue napkin printed with horseshoes
and a pair of dice, snake eyes
against your good luck. The bar's
a dive, but the wine's good, red
as god's blood, severed heads
of grapes pressed into foamy must
and sour ferment that—expensive
as this vintage is, its deep perfume,
its oily legs lollygagging down
the glass so slow you can't not think
of the love you're trying to forget—
that readies you for a good brawl,
for the next sip or strangled
song, for the moon-bright
cue ball slamming into the rack.

ILA

> Maybe I should wear lipstick, too.
> —Lemuria

i. Kissing Kurt

On a dare, I kissed
Kurt full on the lips.
"Ewwww!" said
a girl, twisting
her fake taffeta skirt.
And that was all.
The ball skipped
through the two-
square court.
Kids wound up,
threw fists
at the tether
ball winding
the tall pole.
They tossed marks
for hopscotch
on hot asphalt.
They leaped.

ii. Ampelos

A click of heels will take me far
from home, far from all this cock
and bull, thick necks and chew
and lite beer dollar night, far
from girls who know to know

their place, far from pickup trucks'
red brake lights to drunk embrace—
one click and shine in moonlight
and now I'm both tonight,
dancing in gold lamé high heels,
turning slow in blood red wine light.

MARDUK

> What is happening now has significance—in these surroundings.
> —Ludwig Wittgenstein, *Philosophical Investigations*, 583

White wood siding wraps both storeys, tall chimney, barn out back, a horse, a few white chickens with red wattles and gold and black eyes the bull snakes get after at their peril, old GMC flatbed to haul equipment or crops, old house big enough for everybody to get along, you'd think, its paradise of pocket knives in junk drawers and Crisco cans and a thin layer of white lead paint over arsenic-laced wallpaper still peeking out here and there all green and gold and shimmery, and stars settle into patterns on both sides of night no matter who owns the house or how deep the flood and they chase each other till morning,

and some of us on couches and some in sleeping bags on the floor in the den, grownups get the bedrooms, and *we can't sleep we can't sleep* we know where Grandma hides the hard candy. Ghost and monster tales break up the insults—"Four eyes!"—and he'd seethe and we'd dare him to hang out the window or sneak out and throw a rock at the barn door, so when the horse neighed everyone awake Grandma said she'd whup his ass good. But his daddy took up for him and we settled back into whispers and giggles, except Four Eyes turned crabapple red and ran upstairs, mad at Grandma for sitting up in her room all the time and yelling through the door, Grandpa for sleeping and never waking up. Came back with some outlandish pewter plate an uncle'd won at the county fair belted to his chest, fireplace poker in one hand. Said he cut her right in half and threw her out the window. Said one side fell into the dirt; the other flew up in a twister. We'd see in the morning. We'd see, all right. Scared shit out of us. Never teased him again.

SPES

> Is hope a feeling?
> —Ludwig Wittgenstein, *Philosophical Investigations*, 545

The cat wailing is not her cat,
but she sets down her roses
and goes out, the night warm,
looks for the damn thing down
the road where it's curled up
after a fight to lick. She checks
night's ever thinning rage
of light, wishing for a rope
of fire to gather her up
somehow, each late thought
held like a scratchoff
in a liquor store parking lot,
no rush to reveal its numbers
against the moonshine
jar of this tight-lidded town,
but there's some kind
of leaving out ahead,
some way to add
to the chaos, something
more than just this
sick, quiet purring.

HARPOCRATES

> And yet I did not say it.
> —Ludwig Wittgenstein, *Philosophical Investigations*, 637

Staying quiet's not the same as having nothing to say, finger pressed to lips read wrong, read as keeping something in, not out. Let your eyes, a sun and squinting moon, do the talking; let the sorry rose dry petal by falling petal into the empty basin of that last transgression, hands on her thinking she was still in control, the bright center, his sweet girl, his blue, blue Nile. Thing is, that falcon heard the falconer just fine, but just kept flying, thing in its beak still wriggling.

SUD

> Though the ether is filled with vibrations the world is dark.
> —Ludwig Wittgenstein, *Philosophical Investigations*, II vii

Fever of
      wind over
the escarpment blasts   the low
      places, presses cursives of
sand across roads
      into fences, car paint,   eyes
shut against its cutglass   attack and cats
in the culverts hide   and blown
      branches whip, scratch
faces, shoulders,   this
      fever pressing into
the land seeking
a path to
      the underworld, each gust
    a kiss for who's   buried beneath,
what death she   unearths, what lust she
will raise, what awful
      moon brought out   to tug
at the dark
      waters.

XIUHTECUHTLI

> I shall get burnt if I put my hand in the fire: that is certainty.
> That is to say: here we see the meaning of certainty.
> —Ludwig Wittgenstein, *Philosophical Investigations*, 474

Alligator time so light settles into turquoise on the evening horizon wherever some sea heats into fine mist over the marsh. You got to burn it good, girl. Throw a shrimp in grab it back out. Clam or corncob. How long before anything burns is the trick, child magic of finger through flame, stink of arm hair singed. Chopstick it with two pieces of driftwood but it's no good, all charred on top. Bonfire volcanoes red sparks when a log falls or you throw a pinecone in. Smokes the eyes. You got to let it die so you can see the fireworks later. Get right under for the grand finale. Feel it on your skin when it's done, when fireburst turns all ash and falls out over dead hot waves that show off a yellow slash of moon before they break.

WENDOVER

> —The future is hidden from us.
> —Ludwig Wittgenstein, *Philosophical Investigations*, II xi

Descend from the pass into the high desert, flat sink between home and home, bone white lines on a road that stays where it is to divide salt from salt a sea abandoned to this wind. At night, lights on the horizon tremble, glitter of The Apollo at the border always open and you have to stop, park your fading Lincoln between two radioactive trucks and a latter day Phemonoe swears you have the eyes of a winner and follows you in, pulls you to a table, whispers into your ears into the pips of your dice her prophecy in gambler's hexameter *you will win you will win you will win* her ecstasy explains *you will win* and your dice rattle *you will win* and your last wrinkled dollar promises *you will win* and the desert rises up, a fire against all this night, this night that fades into a table of empty tumblers and crumpled cocktail napkins, *Do you*, she asks, *want to get out alive?*

SUB ROSA

> Two pictures of a rose in the dark. One is quite black; for the rose is invisible.
> —Ludwig Wittgenstein, *Philosophical Investigations*, 515

still life in the blackout dark of a hot room
book black on the black desk the pen
double black its ink its every word
each black page filled your breath
filling the black air reading aloud
to silence to the dark's black shape
the black floor black walls black the shut
door each black picture traced by a hand
reaching for the black rose
its black vase caught in the frame
black reaching for the nymph
hidden beside the black shape
of the rose she was killed to become

EURYPHAESSA

> One did not see before what is now in focus.
> —Ludwig Wittgenstein, *Philosophical Investigations*, 645

Sun on the water shatters
to its spray of gold, a face
under it, my boy's, my girl's
a moon at night a shining
the current can't carry away,
no dawn to awaken them.

That my own brother . . .
There can be no time but this
pacing the bank, tearing hair,
cursing this seeing, unable
to stop looking for light
in their wet, open eyes.

STATIONS OF THE CROSS

> How can there be so much as a temptation here?
> —Ludwig Wittgenstein, *Philosophical Investigations*, 277

Behind St. John's, crude crosses
with numbered labels scatter
down the slope toward the creek,
interrupt a bike trail
into woods to the mill pond
past hollows where kids gather,
smoke, drink, try things they think
are grown up, their teenage
Via Dolorosa past this cheerless
Scout project untended, ignored,
except when kids push through on bikes
or when I look for chanterelles
among weeds under oaks.

                         Once
a cottonmouth guarded station eight.
I watched for an hour, expectant
like Eve for it to speak, to offer
passage to that other world,
but it sulked, ignored me, slithered
finally back toward the brush
beside the damp creek bank, paradise.

III.
WHAT YOU CANNOT SAY

HAT
For my brother, Todd.

Artichoke leather, wide brim
to keep Coos Bay rain off
the face—or sun—no roll,
slim braided leather bond, your sweat
still stains the band, pinch slight
and the crown flat,
a solid hat to wear
salmon season pulling kings
out of the Coquille
to smoke and grill
to relieve your stress
from work trimming firs.

Until you were hung out
by a boss who hated
your union line,
spurred and harnessed, you'd
hang clipped to lines
a hundred feet up
and watch the grounded
world as an osprey might.

I hold it in my hand.
You put a bullet
in your head. Beloved
smell of leather, cigarette
smoke, what I have of you
to hold. I won't. . .
I can't put it on.

CALLIOPES

For Peter Everwine and Philip Levine.

In your back yard, mulberry tree in full
summer shag, vines up a lattice
beside the table, we sip wine,
speak of your lost best friend, Phil.
"It was hard." All you could say:
the cancer, what it took from your heart,
from his last days, from all of us.

In the silence that must follow,
two hummingbirds break
from the tree, sip
red syrup from a feeder,
zip back into the shag.
"Calliopes! Two!" you point,
noting the green back, the purple-
red beard, your tired voice delighted
now. "I thought there was only one."
"Two muses!" I laugh. "Beautiful!"
"Two," you say, watching, and you smile,
begin a funny story about Phil.

ÉLEVAGE

For Mark Strand.

pumped over stems and skins, black must
foams till sweet scent sours right

where you went I called after with fire
in my eye, your false name on my lips

wine on white tile, sinked plates and cups
and flatware, bottles, spall of an evening

rain, too, you seem to think, will raise
anything to absence and gorgeous ruin

hold it in one hand, rest its spine
under light enough to shape its black

moon is m and n and oo, is moan and know,
new and fool enough for every poem, you addict

FEAR OF WATER, 19Ø3

For Nana.

the rabid dog breaks through the barbed wire
and your dad has to get his gun and shoot it
while you hide under the porch
because you know he has to shoot it and everything
it bites, even you in your Sunday best
scared in the dirt under the slats
the sun breaks through in gold lines
across your dress, across the bow you tied
so carefully because you'll go into the house
of God and that bow your real prayer
said before anyone could see you, before the dog
and before Mama smiled, straightened it,
before your papa blasted the hound to oblivion
and blasted your own bit and whimpering
and your hand clutching the lace the light gracing your wrist
and all you can say in the full presence of the Lord
and the body assembled and held together
beneath the slats upon the dust under the dark porch
and the pews of light and your hand upon the knotted lace
holding the body together against madness and time
and your late blue eyes, telling me, tying again this perfect bow.

BONE WINE
For my grandfather.

Unpruned vines bend to earth
Early winter in Paso Robles,
When rain spills into the chalk
And loam between black roots and fists
Of antediluvian bone.
I found, set beside a black oak's
Mossy trunk, one hacked vertebra,
Gone to mineral and grey as paper
All these million years. The bone
Drank up the downpour, or seemed to,
Thirsty from holding up all dead
And living ages of the dust.

I brought it home ten years ago,
And now I drink the wine that grows there,
Hold up the glass to watch the living
Light shimmer, and keep a hallowed place
To rest the used up fossil, save it
Like a river stone. But my grandfather,
Himself now bone and paper,
He'd have kicked it into the vines,
Cursed it, scolded, "Get back to work."
And it would've.

THOTH
For Richard Beban.

Can we choose one at pleasure? (The Egyptian, for instance.)
    —Ludwig Wittgenstein, *Philosophical Investigations* II, xii

Tannin-darkened water shimmers wiregrass
and reed blades mirroring down beside the groaning
walkway out to the viewing tower. Pitcher
plants yawn. Spanish moss laces tupelo
and cypress stands, knees pushing
into knurled islands. And damselflies in the heat hover
and green anoles rush along the handrails.

Most want to see an alligator, but you've
come for birds—warblers, towhees,
great herons, scarlet tanagers—you hope to see
over the dark waters. You point and make
the swamp alive for me with naming, then stop
quiet and point at a white figure in the near distance
dipping into the dark, lifting with its curled neck
a head with a long, down-curved orange beak.
"Is that an ibis? I've never seen one in the wild!"
and you marvel at its hieroglyphic grace, its long
slow step, the way it writes on the wet black page.

THE TEMPLE

> As fire is covered by smoke, as a mirror is covered by dust, or as the embryo is covered by the womb, the living entity is similarly covered by different degrees of lust.
> —*Bhagavad Gita* 3:38 (tr. Christopher Isherwood)

i.

Night fragments into so many stories over India that I have to see
if you still sit looking beside me in the bicycle rickshaw at all
the spires and minarets of places we won't sleep that night,
at strings of lights from wedding festivals, at puddles shimmering
in roads of dust and ashes fallen from pyres burnt beside the river.
And the dark sway of an elephant musks the air with a burden of scent
that might be camel or horse or oxen in another country.

But these are only comparisons, drawn beneath the same stars—Pleiades, Pollux,
Deneb—under the same stone moon which, earlier, crushed its manganese light
through the stench of Calgary slaughterhouses and humid Dallas smog.
so none of this is new, and the shadow of the elephant has passed by anyway,
and I may have just confused its odor with the drying pats of cow dung
mixed with straw, the cooking fuel that lines the mud walls
running beside the tracks through Benares, back toward Calcutta.

So I have nothing to say, and can only point—a weary, inarticulate guide—
at more minarets and spires drawn beneath a moon I recognize
vaguely, and can even name, *moon*, with the stone my tongue has become,
but I can't name the hotel I've read of in the guide, so the driver pedals us
to someplace modern and dark, looming tall and windowed awkwardly
in this dim light where we surrender beneath a slow fan wobbling above
to the exhaustions of journey, to a quick conversion from dollars to rupees,
to a sudden diffidence with words, with bodies, this burden of so many stars.

ii.

Before the sun comes up, a gecko does push-ups for love against the mirror
and greets us with a pair of nods. I am pleased to say *morning* and *gecko*,
but you still sleep, and the lizards find their opposite ways down the glass
until one disappears into the carpet's weave of animals hidden
in leaves and vines, and the other just disappears.

I push you awake so we'll be in time for the Ganges tour,
so we'll be in time to witness the horror or beauty
we expect friends to ask about when we get home. We keep a log
smudged with penciled words and drawings, so when we visited
other countries for the first time, we would try their words for beauty—
Bellissima at Roman fountains and portraits in museums,
or *Wundersam*, or *magnifique*. But in India we settled for *beauty*
and satisfied ourselves by placing *oppressive* before it, a talisman
against the heat, against the staring eyes of those who carried
their burdens of the dead to burn at the river's *ghats*.

So when we step into the wobbly boat, we are not prepared to witness
the river and its bloated eye of sun rising over distant cut-out fronds
of jungle palms, rising above sandstone temples and mosques beside the river
that shines beneath the black boats plying a slow current laced with ash and cries
of bathers massed on shore, waiting to cleanse themselves in the pure
river of the dead and living. All the while, smoke spires rise from the bank,
and we are silent.

I can't put any of these visions in the small, brass vase I bargained down
to twenty rupees as we ride the tour bus to the next stop, the Monkey Temple.
Your reflection wavers, distorted on the urn against the curving curtain
of trees on the horizon, or maybe it is confused or angry at the face behind you
trying to peer into the space between the nape of your neck and the shirt
you've loosened against the heat, against the oppressive beauty
of four thousand years, of so many souls rising into fire-thickened sky.

iii.

As we walk to the Monkey Temple, we check our cameras
while the guide speaks rapidly about Krishna and the monkeys,
about the uncleanness our shoes carry, so we take them off
before we climb the steps to look for rhesus monkeys,
spires, golden statues, and paintings like and unlike many
we have seen elsewhere, but which we are paying to see.

So when I take a picture on the stairs, I call you down to look
at a monkey holding her dead baby like a doll, and she screams
at me because I might take her baby instead of this picture
of her madness, of her rag of a child smiling stone teeth for me
after so many months in the humid, jungle air.

There is so little left for me to take, I wonder if it's the heat that makes her
stop and try to nurse what becomes a lighter burden in her arms,
nurturing what only grows truly dead and held tightly against all
catastrophe this temple excuses to the light. She holds on,
even against the heat, even against her child's tightening smile.

iv.

If we had seen the woman shopping at a Texas grocer's,
picking out casaba or tomato, thumbing a rind, scoring skin
with a nail for something firm and ripe and living inside,
we wouldn't have noticed that she had carried something dead
inside her until it turned into a kind of stone.

Later she might stare through the coffee shop window,
and the rain would wash the curb with gasoline iridescence,
and the letters would turn their backs on anyone
who might come inside for a cup of lousy coffee—free refills.

She would wonder at her childlessness and remember students in tight rows
that failed to contain their nervous laughter when she taught them, in Health,
names like *epididymus*, fallopian tube, *vas deferens*, *Mons Veneris*—
the mountain of love—spoken in perfect Latin to the lucky girls
whose parents signed goldenrod slips because they didn't think
that the body, fossilized in dead languages, could be resurrected
by the archaeology of fingers pressing for something living inside.

The coffee by now would be tepid, and her late husband—
who'd finally consented to a test and was fertile, and at whom she smiles
just now, remembering he never blamed her and nights would kiss her
low on the belly, as though having a child was still possible into their sixties—
he would have laughed at the irony of such a monument to fatherhood,
blamed it, she imagines, on his rock-hard manhood until he'd get to the part
where it was a girl, and he would name her Lois or Arlene in the small fiction
she invents while gazing into the stainless-steel instruments.

When she removes her surgical gown in the small room so she can dress,
she can't decide whether Tuesday or Wednesday would be better to give birth
to her fossil child, perhaps because she won't be able to eat the night before,
or because death has had such a long gestation inside of her
she's reluctant to give it up despite the pain.

v.

Neither my wife nor I can decide whether our daughter was conceived
in the Hong Kong Ritz by the shadowed blue of the BBC talk show
or in our San Francisco apartment among the unsteady moments
between bank account and employment while lights outside quaked
from cars and voices too full of the city. Because any conception
loses the memory of its origin, we fall back on the sciences
of ultrasound and math to trace a sequence invented after the fact.

But she's downstairs right now writing at the desk you gave us, Larry,
pressing the bones of her hand to pen a story of her life without having to lie,
and she is succeeding, I fear, to weave something I will never understand,
something that can't be threaded back to me or traced to any stone
that I might leave behind for her to hold against the loss of my soul,
or whatever eddies up from dust or fire or water, or from her simple act
of breathing as she concentrates on the next, perfect word.

vi.

On the outskirts of Calcutta, I pass a man dead or dying on the hot dust
of a wide and empty road, and I do not know whether to shoo the flies
from his open sores, or to add to the coins which have blossomed
around his body. I do not know the fare for such a journey, so I bet
against doubt with the flower-shaped coin I toss to buy his fire.

I have erased, so many times from this poem, the word *soul*
because soul is what is lost in these transactions between fire and sky,
lost to photos taken of smoke, lost in all that memory loses,
so that soul becomes what I use to explain all that I've lost,
and because of all that I keep losing, I suppose my soul is inexhaustible.

Eddies of ash lighten currents swirling in the wide, sun-streaked river every morning,
and thin reeds of smoke from funeral pyres write nothing on the rising humid air.
And all these rivers that we stand beside, these fires that we burn—
they aren't the beginnings or the ends of anything.

LOOKING FOR CAFÉ MIDI: FRESNO, 1983

Trying to find the old café, I'd found instead a Vietnamese restaurant. The hoisin grilled pork was good and cheap, but I was after cappuccino, chasing a memory of when my cousin, Jim, nurturing my interest in chess, would lend me books on the game along with garishly covered Ace double sci-fi titles to read. He took me just once to the café to hang out, play, watch the old guys feed their camels to the smoky air and snap each piece to threaten from its square. No talk. They'd slap the chess clock after every move. They seemed angry and the "hippies," my father would have called them, mad, too, talking politics in, I'm guessing, 1971, Vietnam and Nixon, sharp coffee smells breaking through the smoke and clatter, the cool marble table holding up the board and our cups. It all baffled me then, but I craved it when I moved back, wanted a place to be strange and sip coffee and argue, listen, or just watch, but it was gone, along with the ghosts I sought, talk of poets and dreamers who'd passed through and left something in the air, some phrase to catch, some kind of anarchy out of the narrowing grid I'd found myself confined in then. Instead, bean thread in spring rolls, rice, first taste of pho and fish sauce. And now I miss that, too.

LAST AUBADE

Because love is not enough and we fail it anyway,
there's nothing to do but trace the wide curve of your hip as you sleep beside me,
nothing to hear but your breath and the cries of crows outside
scrabbling over whatever crumbs the stars will leave in the twisting cypress branches,
and the panoply of stars distracts us from love's magnitude,
and we fail again to listen to the crows in their dark branches
cawing at us to behold the one thing greater than all the darkness they contain.

There's nothing to do but get up and walk out quietly so I don't wake you,
so I don't scare away the light from the Pleiades which guards the bowl of your room
from the sounds of a hinge squeaking, from a gate banging shut.
I walk down the hill one last time, because, after this night,
love will no longer be enough to save us from each other.

TOO MUCH
For Larry Levis.

—And if you are surprised at our playing such a game I refer you to the
effect of a past experience (to the fact that a burnt child fears the fire).
—Ludwig Wittgenstein, *Philosophical Investigations*, 480

Two boys issue a giggling commentary on the joy of anything burning,
too much, under sycamores and the slate-hued winter sky.
Smoke palls and gathers over the boys poking a pile of leaves with branches
under a canopy of branches, pulling a spark or flame to hold out,
to scribble with that spark a phrase against the green canvas of the house before them.

And the boys are you and I, and a car drives past towing the slow hiss of its leaving,
and leaves scatter behind it, and the rakes have given up,
and piles of leaves lie gathered and burning beside the street to ash and smoke,

so we're caught together in the longing of boys, in their words repeated over and over,
too much,
about nothing, and—pointing at the trees, the houses, the wires, the crows along the wires,
the street—about everything.

These two words are all we ever say to each other,
two words, *too much*, we chant until meaning dissolves like smoke into the iron sky,
chant until we make a cult of fall and youth and fire
and all the bounty of ash and dust settling and rising in the forming evening fog.

After you leave, I squat beside the fire and say over and over into the dark
and to a leaf I pick up burning to lace in my small hand—*too much*.
I blow it to ash and absence, taste in this gritty air the good cold dark.

IV.
YOU MUST GIVE

GAME

> Imagine the duck-rabbit hidden in a tangle of lines.
> —Ludwig Wittgenstein, *Philosophical Investigations*, II xi

Saying *this* and intending
    the rain,
        white flowers
of your stretching
    automaton, body
as soul, mix
of words,
        senseless,   once
an expanse of   pond
        amid urban
sprawl reflecting steel   wool
    of fog, red kale
nibbled in
    a community
garden, purple carrots, rainbow
chard, hopeful
    spaniel   and *move*
    in the weeds and *splash*
at the shore   and a wake
through green
    scum   and the
        water
bottle gently
    scudding and once
this
    and intending
        a trowel in
    the furrow,
rush   of movement   the dog off
    after whatever
        it
was you   say you
    saw.

$$EI\, w''''(x) - (H + h(w))\, w''(x) + q/H\, h(w) = p(x)\ \forall x \in (0, L)$$

> A comparison: texts are sometimes hung on the wall. But not theorems of mechanics.
> —Ludwig Wittgenstein, *Philosophical Investigations* II, xi

A handmade paper bears the scars of the poem's text, "from girder into street noon leaks" and "immaculate sigh of stars" and "Under thy shadow by the piers I waited/ Only in darkness is thy shadow clear." Waited for whom, or what? Some *hashishime* of the Brooklyn Bridge, her burning curse, or his? What soars fails, falls from the deck of the steamer into the widening sea, no bridge to save him, no rope, no iron links forged and hammered by Thangtong Gyalpo's long dead fists. Hart Crane's words are still a joy on the wall, on the matted page's sepia tone. They lift, but only "figures" hints, from its distance, at the gravity of the Melan equation for suspension bridges, how it hangs each passage through New York's glittering sky.

THE UNCERTAINTY PRINCIPLE

You never know, and that's about the size
        of all these questions
Asked of matter. Matter never lies;
        it makes suggestions,
Hints at what it is, or where, or when
        if one concedes
That time is not a particle, a spin
        each chronon bleeds
Across the vast continuum. You look,
        and that's just where,
Of course, the problem starts—your look
        that tries to swear
Allegiance to impartiality
        unburdened by
A metaphysic. A multiplicity
        of guesses ties
A knot around (just where) the answer hides,
        the way a lyric
Bends its words around a silence. To pride
        oneself on Pyrrhic
Wins against blank ignorance is vain.
        The stars shine on
And, outside, bluebirds argue in the vine;
        They know it's dawn.

BLUE

> I can only see, not hear, red and green, —but sadness I can hear
> as much as I can see it.
> —Ludwig Wittgenstein, *Philosophical Investigations*, II, xi

One note over and over troubles the winespun mist red and cheap behind your closed eyes, G high on the guitar's neck till it finds you sliding, the hardwood floor six days' dust deep, wires loose, snaking to speakers set down on the floor and aimed at each other across the space of a head, at each ravened ear, eyes closed against a dark slatted with the bleed of street light and the green band of the old stereo and it doesn't matter if it's Radiohead, Gymnopedie No. 1, or Bessie's "Empty Bed," when it gets to the end you hit "repeat."

LATE

—After an untitled landscape by George Seeley

Where once you bent to lift a paperwhite
from the current after we lay together, dark
now holds along the bank and in the willow's
damp beard. It could be the low moon brushes
the air with its breath, and it could be the slow
tune of its light braids the grey course
of the river. It could be. Or it could be you,
and my eyes have yet to find a place for you
gone, this dark held now along the bank,
under branches burdened with these late desires.

A SIDE OF LOVE

> What is my destiny?
> —Graffito over a urinal, Clermont Lounge, Atlanta

We sit down at the Flying Biscuit to wait
for a table. Steam rises from cups,
from plates of eggs and bacon and grits,
from the hot sidewalk and the white collars of men
with bibles and pamphlets bearing signs damning
men for loving men and women for loving women
because they believe in a man who told us
to love one another. They preach through bullhorns
against women in love and men in love and the rest
who don't care how, while folks meander past
this busy honking corner to the Pride Fest
at Piedmont park. Finally we sit and order
omelets and grits and "A side of Love"
—blackbean cakes, tomatillo salsa,
feta, sour cream, and spears of red onions—
delicious and meatless as lovers walk past
and ignore or persuade or admonish or flip off
these men "with men working that which is unseemly."
I don't hate them for confusing carnality
with the spirit, but that they've confused the two
builds hatred out of love, makes marriage into meat, not breath.

• • •

Last night, we went to the Clermont,
"where all sides collide," the only club
in America that doesn't need a bouncer
on Friday night, a motel basement dive
dingy with age and the weariness we bear into weekends
to drink Jack and Coke and PBR while women dance
and strip to music, revealing everything
about us watching, passing wrinkled dollars, talking
and drinking and smoking so we can forget

how our bodies betray us with every exhalation.
They spanked and bumped and gyred and ground and flirted,
some thirty-year veterans of the ecdysial arts—
Porsche, the suicide girl, no Blondie that night
but I think that was her daughter. The barkeep served quick
and shook her fist at a disrespectful birthday group,
slumming tourists here to laugh at the work
the girls, her friends, do there every night,
the "girls" who thanked each of us who tipped
personally, the girls who said goodbye
when we got up to leave, and one who hugged
and kissed my love on the cheek in thanks.

We felt warm and welcome amid the smoke
and booze and flesh and came back to the bar
from the bathroom with questions and answers, signs from the walls
that made more sense than those the men bear in hate.
"What is my destiny?" I brought back laughing from the john.
She returned from the ladies room with the answer—
which turns through all of this, and us—surrounded
by scrawled silly hearts and peace signs, "Let love rule."

. . .

Now we follow to the park, where people
like ducks and funnel cakes and equality and hate
humidity, not how people love each other.
"I love being a pervert," says a lovely
young woman—tattooed, pierced, bored
with the protest—to friends at the cash machine
as they turn through their recent persecutions.
And you love her too as you turn through this.
Admit it, you love flesh as much as anyone,
its paradise veneer, our weird vertebral
rhapsody wrestling with desire to give up
meat through flesh to breath. Admit it.

INTRASOCIAL DISUNITY IN NEOLIBERAL ECONOMIES

> It is easier to get at a feeling of unfamiliarity and of unnaturalness.
> —Ludwig Wittgenstein, *Philosophical Investigations*, 596

You're somewhere else, an old woman riding one of those electric shopping carts admonishes the cashier—young, exhausted in her green smock—waiting for APPROVED to appear on the small screen. Yes, I am. We wait together for APPROVED on the small screen, me beside my assembled groceries on the conveyor—milk if you must know, celery, bananas, ground organic turkey. Care to say where you really are? Smiling. I will ask for paper not plastic this time. She is tired she says No she hands the receipt to the woman who is still waiting I don't. Smiles back thinly. This is when I notice how weary she is, her red-rimmed eyes. Oh, and organic garlic. This is when the bagger arranges the bouquet of the woman's plastic bags in the basket who is APPROVED and disappointed not to know where the cashier in her mind is. Lacuna with its press of unsavory conflicts romances profligacies interest-rate-inflected anxieties pending diagnosis need to step outside for a smoke wherever she both is and is not. Cat who wants the lid shut tight to stay half alive. Oh, she puts slowly her card in her purse looking at the young woman who looks to me as the disappointed woman rides away toward the hot parking lot. A single Canadian goose rests there on a pile of grass in the landscaping of a median. Did you find everything you need? Yes I say Yes thank you.

YOU MUST CHANGE YOUR LIFE

So you do. You head off into the desert where even the land tries to climb out of the heat, succeeds in blue meadows given to cattle and grass and wiry streams pulsing into dark, trout-filled lakes. Cast a line. Pull it and shake the fly. But the fish are tired of all that nylon and the simple jitter of the bug, tired of sitting there turning pale blue and strung out in warm shallow water, tired of catch and release, catch and release. It's still life, a work of art, ice sculpture, dead marble hand, chia head, still life with an open Swiss Army knife and a frayed fly. Here ya' go little fella.

Spare change in your pocket fills with light if you hold it up to read the dates in the bright noon sun. This is best if you have nothing to spend it on, if the light matters more than anything, so when the line pulls and the bobber bobbles in the water, you are too distracted to set the hook, and everything goes away, happy, bait-filled, scales shimmering like coins you might have painted as a small detail in the study for the tapestry you will weave sometime, time permitting.

Catch and release, and the coins spill into the dust and there are just too many corny songs to listen to, too many memories fading into the asphalt's fading mirage. You drive right through it, every time and without hesitation, even when what you want most in the world is for the car to sink into the shimmering cool abyss so you can find out what's on the other side.

It's still asphalt and the sky dirt and the old silver coins surround the skulls of missing travelers and fish wait to be fished out of the deep, grey sandstone to swim again in displays with carbuncle and pyrite and geodes and quartz crystals and purple amethyst and hematite and steel shoestring nipples and old bottles and railroad spikes. The wind blows box elder leaves into the shape of a rose next to a single blue nickel you leave in the dust, still in this noon sun. To catch you. To release you.

SUWANNEE WATERSHED

> Look at the blue of the sky and say to yourself "How blue the sky is!"
> —Ludwig Wittgenstein, *Philosophical Investigation*, 275

Tricking notes in the late morning sky, first a fake cool the heat rises through into late cumulus, vultures banking in wide arcs and hawks soaring low, ready, while mockingbirds press their wars a song at a time and one frozen heron stares quietly down into the creek the box turtle bumpingly navigates, cicada choirs in the stained glass of a sky always falling, light through branches lifted, and fallen sweetgums ransacked by oysters and angelwings, sweetgums and longleafs and pond cypresses, here the silent ones with one leg keeping land from sliding into water as the Timucua who didn't survive us believed when they had lived here, and blue before and after rains after mist rises blue white, only then will cats uncouple from wheel wells to furl their bodies on concrete and lick and lick and no one steps off a porch and looks up without a hand to hide the sun but the green anole, pumping its red neck for what we call love.

SAINT AUGUSTINE

> See how high the seas of language run here!
> —Ludwig Wittgenstein, *Philosophical Investigations*, 194

Hear you while the ocean tumbles around and cownose rays scare a few in the surf and lightning freights a cloud all the way to downpour. Pulled a wake up the still river and a sea of you to look at all the night long, sweet baby, these blues a frail swell of heat ticking down, choir of cicadas back in the loblollies. Moon thugs night in its sick orange rise over the ever-rising Atlantic, scur of clouds, lacerations of white surf in the wet black and the boats ransack pockets of nets into the hold's yawning hatch to take away. But it's all ours, this moon, the surf, lips of waves, a thousand red-eyed cicadas. We fall into the hum of the air-cooled room, damp light and wine enough to divvy up this loot like thieves. One for me, sweet baby. Two for you.

V.
TO SILENCE

QUIET NIGHT

> *Thought* can be of what is *not* the case.
> —Ludwig Wittgenstein, *Philosophical Investigations*, 95

Not this world, nor the box of wax,
nor autogeny of shining corpse flies
alive upon a fawn in early snow, not
the quiet poems of Lorca's dotage,
nor Plato's perfect forms surrounding, nor
a virgin-born child to bring no world hope,
but blocks and pillars, slabs and beams,
an axe, saw, plow, a loom, this quiet
night, one tallow candle, a loaf of bread,
and wine, two glasses, two plates,
you across this table.

CIRCUIT

> —the rest is dark.
> —Ludwig Wittgenstein, *Philosophical Investigations*, 635

Vacant lot under a few stars and no moon
and dead streetlamps, power out and the rain
thinned to mist rising from asphalt and windows
flickering with candlelight or nothing,

to walk the wet road looking up, line of pines
a dark wave breaking, *the way it must have been*,
I want to think, but a car hisses past
shining a river on the wet road and no owls

hunt from the pecan tree, this pause
in the usual city, this walk a kind of hope
for fraying, till at the end of the street
the trucks grind down the way and gold

lights whirl and spots glam on lines and a crane
lifts someone in a hardhat up, hand raised to all
that power. To turn around and walk back
through the damp air slowly. To wait for it.

ESCALANTE

> My glance was vacant; or again *like* that of someone admiring the illumination of the sky and drinking in the light.
> —Ludwig Wittgenstein, *Philosophical Investigations*, 412

Two dead albino coyotes in the back of the ranger's truck in town; he shows them as puzzle, as odd fact. The road to Boulder the kids come down in the yellow school bus every day. From up that way. The body man who puts my car back together asks: "You seen the mountain lion?" It was out at his mother's. He knows I walk the canyons, check the steep walls for petroglyphs, stare and listen, so quiet the red-tailed hawk's wing-beats surprise and echo up Alvey wash. "No," I say. A fossil shark's tooth is all. "Nemo was here" is all at the river, a trickle; finds ways deeper into stone. Slot canyons and stunted cedars under the blue. Or a cold clear winter night and fresh snow, no moon and no one out. The mantled land glows blue from so many stars. To think of the self is to think of not much at all. Walk out into the middle of the road. Look up at the spray of them, crack of ice underfoot, a puzzle.

UTAH

> But "knowing" it only means: being able to describe it.
> —Ludwig Wittgenstein, *Philosophical Investigations*, II, viii

If nothing happens, still the bowl of mountains thrusts into the desert twilight, first star in the blue between two peaks, if you are in the bowl, the valley darkening, fallen, or resting perhaps, looking up at the peaks like teeth, sharp as a goth-girl's filed to fangs and she smiles to show them to you and nobody else, or they rather flatly rise, not thrusting at all, like new teeth pushing through the gums of a baby's lower jaw, your baby, drool leaking onto your T-Rex shirt as the baby sweetly sleeps finally and you gaze at her cowlick, strands shimmering in red highlight beneath the lamp turning slightly on its chain above, the lamp a star above a desert valley, peaks robed in twilight, this narrow road you know so well.

HIGH DESERT

Nothing's been in the rearview mirror so long that I finally adjust it until my eye settles on the glint and wobble of headlamps or stars on the flat desert horizon. It's the same sheen a child focuses on, lying on hot cement in the back yard after running through the sprinkler's wet rainbow over the lawn. Stars of each drop glisten on blond hairs invisible in most light, and each star blurs to arc-lamp snowflakes flaring sun-white over concrete. Get up, leave the wet outline of a body on the ground like the small white tag beside the thorny pyracantha to tell anyone forever how to care for it.

By now it's 105 degrees and tires bend to it, melt into the road even this late where a giant neon thermometer promises good food and respite from each of these words. The lime-green antifreeze in the parking lot gives up to the oil-spotted asphalt and the pay phone rings anyway and nobody is there to answer except Nate and Abe, who apologize for being the wrong people and laugh at the adventure of picking up a phone suddenly ringing in the middle of nowhere. Everything evaporates. The oil. The antifreeze. The wet outline of a child's body. The ringing phone. Each memory I have of this coffee steam swirling up into the ceiling fan and the waitress asking how I can drink it in this heat. So I begin to tell her the only thing anyone can tell her when it's this hot and she's been standing there so long and so lovely against the din of the phone and the silence of formica, but it evaporates too before her chin turns toward the thick-armed cook, who calls out that all the orders are ready right now, and she serves them. The coins glisten and glisten, but cool nothing on the counter beside the foil-wrapped chrysanthemum.

Stars shimmer and wane in the dead-bug arc the wipers never reach, and for each, here or on a boy's wet, tanned arm, this spectrum's for you: sodium, cobalt, nickel, carbon, helium, hydrogen, argon, manganese, asphalt, soft shoulder, stink thistle, ragweed, 12 gauge, hollowpoint, blown tire, Indio 53 miles, double yellow, slippery when wet, falling rock . . .

VIRGA

> We see the straight highway before us, but of course we cannot use it, because it is permanently closed.
> —Ludwig Wittgenstein, *Philosophical Investigations* 426

House sold and settled and a week to clear it all out, load the 26-foot U-Haul alone, miss Kim hard, think of my wife, our separation and will it last, our children tangled in their vanishing childhoods and our mess, coyotes in the canyon and the wine glass I left for them, for the memory, what here I'll leave and what to carry on other than books and furniture, a last night sleeping on the hardwood and up into the dry salt weather of morning and its promise of road food all that desert day, past the mountains, truck stops, past Mesquite and sand and scrub, sky lit with glare and a fraying cloud and rain falling, but never finding ground.

NOR SPANISH NOR MOSS

beard bromeliad
white fall
of city oaks
down canopy roads

ghost silver winters
in swamp cypresses
black water
mirrors and mist
unsettles vultures

what wires tangle
what your tiny bell
flowers have seen
and rung out

LATE THUNDERSTORM

> One is inclined to say: "Either it is raining, or it isn't—how I know, how the information has reached me, is another matter."
> —Ludwig Wittgenstein, *Philosophical Investigations* 356

The light remains steady
despite all this. The fan
winds its rotation of shadows
across the planked ceiling.

The darkened double panes
reflect the light above,
doubled, and I am a blur
of two across the room.

Night enters through
lightning strikes, then
thunder, and the rain
gathered in a stream

falls from the roof valley
and clatters against the brick
that I want to say I know
is outside, but you never

know in the philosophy
of rain unless you run
through it toward a small
awning under a lamp

to wait it out, to feel
the cool damp against
the stucco wall until
the pavement steams.

WINTER NIGHT

> Back to the rough ground!
> —Ludwig Wittgenstein, *Philosophical Investigations*, 107

Keeping no night away, the one bergamot candle lit in the window, for Eros, for wine in the dim glass on the table beside a spatchcocked book, a faint and unremarkable music—unless the quiet of it all pulls a shadow, darkens the panes, unless this door opens, unless the threshold bears one up against the flickering—one step, then another, one house, a block of houses, a street corner under all its flashing, urgent air and another, chill of crusty snow at the ankle, and another, and no one follows on the cracking pavement.

ENVOI

SLAB!

> And to imagine a language means to imagine a form of life.
> —Ludwig Wittgenstein, *Philosophical Investigations*, 19

Heavier than you can carry, marble
or granite or heart pine or fire-tempered
Troncais thick to raise a palace
or a fort, raised to fill a doorway, slab
of heavy oak fit to a warship hull,
of iron to the prison wall hung
with rusted shackles, leveled and laid
to ground to seal off hell from the nave
from the chancel from the transept
from the choirs, slab cold on bare feet
and the children run, slab off the glacier
in the bay until it all melts, poured concrete
into tract after tract of You could be home
right now! and the children run, thick cut
of beef, bacon, dark rye, sharp cheddar,
butter, slab on slab on slab on slab,
dry-rubbed and smoked, Memphis
or Kansas City or Georgia baby backs
or St. Louis, Texas brisket slab, toe to it,
pitch inside or down the pipe, goofy-footed
kook bailin' a bitchin' slab in a tight barrel,
spinning that Hendrix blues slab 33 1/3
through your first perfect kiss, or
slow low and bangin' V-8 Olds Cutlass
to the 110 easy all the way to Slab City
to check out East Jesus unless the blue light
sprays the rearview, just say it and we'll go.

NOTES

Section headings are a translation of the first and last proposition of Wittgenstein's *Tractatus Logico Philosophicus* (Harcourt, Brace & Company, Inc. 1922): *1 Die Welt ist alles, was der Fall ist. 7 Wovon man nicht sprechen kann, duruber muss man schweigen.* The liberties taken with the translation presume Wittgenstein intended them also to be read as a poem in addition to statements about language and its limits, so "Fall," typically translated as "Case" in English, is here rendered as the Fall, privileging its other German meaning. Rendered as a poem, it scans roughly as iambic dimeter, rhymes, and features a silent (or blank, in writing) final foot.

> *Die Welt is alles,*
> *was der Fall ist.*
> *Wovon man*
> *nicht sprechen kann,*
> *daruber muss man*
> *schweigen.*

"Writing Spider: (Argiope Aurantia)": Orb weaver that builds a web with a striking stabilimentum that looks like writing. The folktale about the spider's ability to predict the number of years a smiling viewer has left to live was recorded as told to me by my former student, Taylor Patterson, and the recording was used in both the Califone album *All My Friends are Funeral Singers* and the movie of the same title by Tim Rutili.

"Ixchel": Maya Jaguar Goddess of tokology, and by extension, fertility and medicine, but other affiliations include the moon, mutability, war, and artistic creation, including weaving. According to the *Ancient History Encyclopedia*, contemporary images of her have been "conflated . . . with the Virgin Mary."

"Nit": Egyptian goddess, creator of the universe through seven spoken words and affiliated with wisdom, war, birth, death, and weaving.

"Desire": Kamadeva is the Hindu god of desire, and Rati is his wife. He is affiliated with spring, symbolized in part by his parrot that serves in some images as his mount.

"Hunahpu": One of the Maya Hero Twins famous for their ability at Poc-a-Toc, the "game of the gods," who defeated the underworld gods and resurrected their father, killed for disturbing the underworld deities with noise from the ball game.

"Shezmu": Egyptian god of wine, excess, inebriation and perfume, who tormented the souls of the damned by crushing their heads like shiraz grapes.

"Ila": Hindu deity, gender-shifting mother and father of the Lunar dynasty. Lemuria is an outstanding punk band originally from Buffalo, NY.

"Marduk": Babylonian king of gods and creator of humans, slayer of his grandmother Tia-Mat, who led forces of chaos against her own children.

"Spes": Roman goddess of hope. When Pandora opened her box, she alone remained behind to help mankind. She is affiliated with flowers.

"Harpocrates": Greek god of silence, a misinterpretation of the Egyptian god of the sun Horus, son of Osiris and Isis, who as a child was often depicted with his finger to his lips. One story has Eros bribing Harpocrates with a rose from Aphrodite to keep her illicit dalliances secret.

"Sud": Mesopotamian goddess seduced or in some versions raped by Enlil, who marries her to make amends. Nevertheless, they are condemned to the underworld, where Enlil masquerades as a guard at the gates, and Sud/Ninlil offers herself sexually to him to gain entrance in order to join Enlil. She is mother of several important gods and goddesses, including the moon god, Nanna.

"Xiuhtecuhtli": Aztec god of fire and time (heat, the day, volcanoes), whose name comes from the Aztec word for turquoise, which also means "year," and also lord of the first hour of night, named after the Aztec word for "alligator."

"Wendover": Phemonoe is a poet and first Pythia of the Oracle of Delphi and daughter of Apollo (or his son, Delphus). The invention of hexameter verse is attributed to her.

"Sub Rosa": In Greek mythology, Chloris, goddess of spring and flowers, found the body of a nymph and, with the help of several gods and goddesses, transformed her into a rose. See also the note to "Harpocrates" above.

"Euryphaessa": Also, Thea, Titan goddess of sight who bore Helios (the sun) and Selene (the moon). The brother is Kronos.

"Thoth": Egyptian god of the moon, writing, equilibrium, and wisdom, his images were rendered with the head of an ibis.

"$EI\ w''''(x) - (H + h(w))\ w''(x) + q/H\ h(w) = p(x)\ \forall x \in (0, L)$": Engineers employ the Melan equation in suspension bridge design. Quoted lines are from Hart Crane's "To Brooklyn Bridge." *Hashishime* is a Japanese bridge demon goddess (*oni*). Fifteenth century Buddhist master Thangtong Gyalpo is credited with inventing the suspension bridge.

Quotations from Ludwig Wittgenstein's *Philosophical Investigations* are from the third edition published by Basil Blackwell Ltd, Oxford.

ACKNOWLEDGMENTS

Many thanks to editors who first published versions of the poems that make up this book.

Journals

"A Side of Love": *Chattahoochee Review*
"Roast" and "Quiet Night": *Hubbub.*
"Oyster" from "Fungus Suite" and "Saint Augustine": *Journal of Florida Studies*
"Desire," "Spes," "Euryphaessa," "Stations of the Cross," "Thoth," "Intrasocial Disunity in Neoliberal Economies," "Circuit," "Nor Spanish Nor Moss," "Late Thunderstorm," and "Suwannee Watershed": *Live Encounters*
"Calliopes," and "Looking for Café Midi: Fresno, 1983": *Miramar*
"The Temple": *New Virginia Review*
"Winter Morning" and "Ceci n'est pas un pot": *Plume*
"Virga," "Game," and "Slab": *Salt*
"Vermeer," "Hunahpu: Panhandle, San Francisco, 1982," "Last Aubade," and "Too Much": *TheScreamOnline*
"Élevage," "Kite," "Escalante": *Western Humanities Review*

Books

"You Must Change Your Life" and "High Desert": *Bear Flag Republic: Prose Poems and Poetics from California* (edited by Christopher Buckley and Gary Young, Greenhouse Review Press 2008)
"Hat": *Composing Poetry: A Guide to Writing Poems and Thinking Lyrically* by Gerry Lafemina (Kendall Hunt 2016)
"Bone Wine": *How Much Earth: The Fresno Poets* (eds. Christopher Buckley, David Oliveira, and M. L. Williams, Roundhouse Press 2001)
"Fear of Water, 19Ø3" and "Late": *Other Medicines* (chapbook by the author; Redbone Press 2008; "Late" was commissioned by the Santa Barbara Museum of Art)
"Summer Thunderstorm": *Stone, River, Sky: An Anthology of Georgia* (Negative Capability Press, 2015)
"The Uncertainty Principle": *Verse & Universe: Poems about Science and Mathematics* (edited by Kurt Brown, Milkweed Editions 1998)

Thanks to wonderful poet-editor Kevin Cantwell at What Books Press for insight and advice, along with Karen Kevorkian, Gail Wronsky, Kate Haake, and book designer Ash Good. I thank Peter Everwine and Andrew Miller for invaluable feedback on earlier versions of the manuscript, and the friends who made suggestions on poems—Kurt Brown, Andrea Rogers Patton, Brooke McKinney, John Guzlowski, Noah Blaustein, and my Santa Barbara workshop: David Oliveira, Barry Spacks, and Chryss Yost. Thanks to amazing teachers for their lessons and encouragement (the mistakes, however, I own), including Fred Caire and Jo Doris Hibner at Fresno High; Robert Pinsky, Thom Gunn, Ron Loewinsohn, Jackson Burgess, Tom Schaub, John Searle, and Rochelle Nameroff at U. C. Berkeley; Peter, Philip Levine, Charles G. Hanzlicek, Corinne Clegg Hales, Jacqueline Doyle, and Ernesto Trejo at Fresno State; and Jacqueline Osherow, Larry Levis, Eavan Boland, François Camoin, Karen Brennan, Robert Caserio, Brooke Hopkins, Barry Weller, Lee Rust Brown, David Kranes, Donald Revell, and Mark Strand at Utah. Thanks to fellow students in the workshops at Fresno State, especially Andrew, Adam Hill, and Loren Palsgaard, and to fellow creative writing students at Utah, especially Craig Arnold, Lawrence Coates, Tom Hazuka, Jeffrey Vasseur, Ann Hudson, Gerda Saunders, Alexander Thorburn, Wendy Rawlings, Donald Platt, Heather Hirschi, Sally Thomas, Jennifer Tonge, Joel Long, Connie Voisine, Thomas Hawks, Amanda Pecor, Dawn Corrigan, Sophia Kartsonis, Tina Johnson, Jan-Ruth White, Julie Turley, Claire Lawrence, Dana Roeser, Kris Jacobson, and Margot Schilpp, whose support and encouragement I value more than they will ever know. Thanks to Ross White's Grind. Thanks to Rick Campbell and Jim White for friendship and Florida community. I thank many writers who've been kind and inspiring along the way—Agha Shahid Ali, Jackson Wheeler, Carolyn Kizer, Chuck Moulton, Lisa Steinman, Jim Shugrue, Albert Goldbarth, Bob Hicok, Dorianne Laux, Andrea Hollander, Robert Wrigley, Yerra Sugarman, Khaled Mattawa, Mark Jarman, Kelly Cherry, T. R. Hummer, Kaaren Kitchell, Richard Beban, Sholeh Wolpe, Tony Barnstone, Charles Harper Webb, Lynne Thompson, Sarah Maclay, Cathy Coleman, Helene Cardona, John Fitzgerald, Jennifer Clough, Kevin Patrick Sullivan, Kevin Clark, Dorothy Barresi, Jim Natal, Marjorie Becker, Roberta George, Deborah Hall, Scott Cairns, Ralph Tejeda Wilson,

Katherine Coles, Bill Coles, Christopher Merrill, Gregory Donovan, Mary Flinn, David Baker, Laure-Anne Bosselaar, Phil Taggart, Marsha De La O, Perie Longo, Valentina Gnup, David Starkey, Glenna Luschei, Amy Esau, Madeleine Sorapure, George Yatchisin, Pam Inglesby, John Ridland, Sandra Beasley, Don Morrill, Lisa Birnbaum, Erica Dawson, Tom Hallock, Lisa Zimmerman, Tania Rochelle, Bob Kunzinger, Jay Snodgrass, Barbara Hamby, David Kirby, Carol Lynne Knight, Jon Tribble, Allison Joseph, Jeff Mock, Mark Ulyseas, Hugh O'Connell, Sarah Hamblin, Jacob Jewusiak, Myrto Drizou, David St. John, Mari L' Esperance, Kathy Fagan, Glover Davis, Jon Vineberg, Dixie Salazar, Frances Levine, Sam Pereira, Suzanne Lummis, Gary Soto, Jefferson Beavers, DeWayne Rail, Marty Paul, Stephen D. Gutierrez, Brian Turner, Heather McHugh, Mark Doty, Gerry LaFemina, Kimberly Kafka, William T. Vollmann, Joy Castro, Eleni Sikelianos, Sharon Dolin, Joyce Jenkins, Stuart Dischell, Tim Rutili, and Kim Addonizio, among so many others. Thanks to Ann Binney and the *Los Angeles Times* for supporting poetry. Thanks to Valdosta State University for institutional support, wonderful colleagues, and amazing students. Thanks also to my wonderful Georgia Poetry Circuit colleagues. This book is also dedicated to the memory of my late brother's sweet, beautiful son Erick, who left us much too young. I dedicate this to my children, Ian and Elizabeth, both scientists, for putting up with a poet father, to my two beautiful Australian granddaughters, Freya and Elise and their father James, and to Alice's children John and Victoria. Thanks to my parents for love and for buying me hundreds of books when I was young. Most of all, I dedicate this book to Alice Cox for love and dance, chemistry and inspiration.

M. L. WILLIAMS is author of the chapbook *Other Medicines* and co-editor of *How Much Earth: The Fresno Poets*, and he served as editor or co-editor of *Quarterly West* for five years. His work is in many journals and anthologies, including *Plume, Hubbub, Salt, Western Humanities Review, Miramar, The Journal of Florida Studies, The Cortland Review, Live Encounters Poetry*, and *Stone, River, Sky*, and has been nominated for several Pushcart Prizes. He co-emcees the Poetry Stage at the Los Angeles Times Festival of Books, and he teaches creative writing and contemporary literature at Valdosta State University.

LOS ANGELES

OTHER TITLES FROM WHAT BOOKS PRESS

ART

Gronk, A Giant Claw
Bilingual, spanish

Chuck Rosenthal, Gail Wronsky & Gronk,
Tomorrow You'll Be One of Us: Sci Fi Poems

PROSE

François Camoin, *April, May, and So On*

A.W. DeAnnuntis, *The Mysterious Islands and Other Stories*

Katharine Haake, *The Time of Quarantine*

Mona Houghton, *Frottage & Even As We Speak: Two Novellas*

Rod Val Moore, *Brittle Star*

Chuck Rosenthal, *Coyote O'Donohughe's History of Texas*

NON-FICTION

Chuck Rosenthal, *West of Eden: A Life in 21st Century Los Angeles*

POETRY

Kevin Cantwell, *One of Those Russian Novels*

Ramón García, *Other Countries*

Karen Kevorkian, *Lizard Dream*

Gail Wronsky, *Imperfect Pastorals*

WHATBOOKSPRESS.COM

www.ingramcontent.com/pod-product-compliance
Lightning Source LLC
Chambersburg PA
CBHW020544080526
44583CB00013B/980